POULTRY ON THE FARM

Cliff Moon

Illustrated by Bill Donohoe

A DOWN ON THE FARM BOOK

THE BOOKWRIGHT PRESS
NEW YORK · 1983

Other books in this series

DAIRY COWS ON THE FARM
SHEEP ON THE FARM
PIGS ON THE FARM

Published in the United States in 1983 by
The Bookwright Press, 387 Park Avenue South, New York NY 10016
First published in 1983 by
Wayland Publishers Ltd., England.
©Copyright 1983 Wayland Publishers Ltd

ISBN: 0-531-04697-4
Library of Congress Catalog Card Number: 83-71631
Printed in Italy by
G. Canale & C.S.p.A., Turin

Contents

Look at the picture.
This family is having breakfast.
They are eating eggs.
Eggs come from poultry, and
this book is about poultry.

Here are four different kinds of poultry.
There is a goose, a turkey, a duck
and some chickens. The picture shows
two kinds of chickens.
Different kinds of poultry
lay different kinds of eggs.
Which do you think are bigger—
hens' eggs or turkeys' eggs?
(Answer on page 32)

Light Sussex
(Chicken)

hen
(female)

cock
(male)

Goose

cock
(male)

hen
(female)

Turkey

Rhode Island Red
(Chicken)

Duck

This hen has laid some eggs in her nest.
Eggs are *oval* shaped so that
they will roll around in a circle.
They cannot roll out of the nest
because of their shape.

It is spring, and the hen
has laid her eggs.
Now she is sitting on them
to keep them warm.
A cock has *mated* with this hen,
so there are tiny chicks
inside her eggs.

There is no cock with these hens.
They will lay eggs without
baby chicks inside.
They lay one egg every day
for about eight months of the year.
Their eggs are the eggs
you buy in a store.

13

Here is a hen with her chicks.
The chicks break the shell with their beaks
when they are ready to be born.
How long do you think the hen
sat on her eggs before they *hatched?*
(Answer on page 32)

The chicks have left their nest, and
the hen is looking after them.
When she sits down, all the chicks
cuddle up under her wings.
The farmer has given them some food.
They eat breadcrumbs or
chopped hard-boiled eggs and shells!

What is happening here?
There is a hen but no chicks!
These are baby ducklings.
Ducks may leave their eggs all alone.
The farmer may have a hen sit on them instead.
When the eggs hatch,
the ducklings jump in a pond.
Chicks don't do that,
so the hen is very upset!

19

These chicks are getting older.
Can you see their feathers?
The farmer is letting them wander around
in the field, but at night he shuts them up
in a poultry house.
Do you know why?
(Answer on page 32)

21

Young hens are called *pullets.*
Here are some pullets.
They have started to lay eggs.
The farmer keeps them indoors
so that they will lay more eggs.
They have food, water and light.
They lay eggs in their *nest boxes.*

Many chicks are born like this
in a *hatchery*.
The eggs are kept in a warm, damp place
until they hatch.

These young chicks are feeding
just like those on page 17.
They have no mother to look after them,
so the farmer keeps them warm
with large heaters.
How many chicks do you think
a farmer can raise
in a building like this?

(Answer on page 32)

These hens have never wandered around
in a field.
They came straight from a hatchery, and
now they live in cages.
They eat, drink, sleep and lay eggs.
The eggs roll down the wire slope, and
the farmer collects them.

29

What is the man doing?
When you have chicken for dinner
you don't want to eat feathers!
The women are packing eggs into boxes
to sell to the stores.
How do you like to eat eggs —
fried, boiled, poached or scrambled?
However you like them,
they all come from poultry.

31

Answers to questions

Page 6

Turkeys' eggs are bigger than hens' eggs.

Page 14

The hen sat on her eggs for 21 days.

Page 20

The farmer shuts the chicks up at night
to stop foxes from eating them.

Page 26

A farmer can raise 20,000 chicks in one building!

Index